I0555161

The CBCT® for Mental Health

Implementation Guide

Bringing Compassion Training into Caring for Mental Health Needs

Center for Contemplative
Science and Compassion-Based Ethics
Emory University

Contents

Introduction

This implementation guide offers key information and strategy for successfully bringing and integrating CBCT for Mental Health into practices and programming that address mental health needs. The main purpose of the guide is to provide a structure to help clinical mental health practitioners enhance and sustain the wellbeing of individuals affected by mental health symptomatology, and to foster a culture of compassion within their practice and organization.

CBCT for Mental Health is a tailored compassion training program aimed at enhancing resilience, compassion, and overall wellbeing. It is designed to equip individuals with practices that support a greater sense of empowerment, inner attunement, exploration, and interconnectedness as they move through their lives. CBCT for Mental Health is an extraordinary approach to personal wellbeing that attends to and serves the whole person, while being mindful of the ongoing impact of mental health symptomatology.

This guide begins with a brief overview of CBCT and how it has been adapted to support mental health. The guide provides insights, recommendations, and resources for implementation in different mental health organizational structures and program types. Through the development of a deliberative and thoughtful plan, and a commitment over time to executing it, CBCT for Mental Health can be implemented in a manner that contributes to the wellbeing of clients, residents, patients, practitioners, providers, colleagues, and staff.

"Compassion is essential for survival. Without cooperation, trust, gratitude, and reciprocity—as well as the many other qualities associated with compassion—humans would not have survived, let alone flourished."

— DACHER KELTNER, *BORN TO BE GOOD: THE SCIENCE OF A MEANINGFUL LIFE*, 2009

Program Overview

CBCT® (Cognitively Based Compassion Training), a program of Emory University's Center for Contemplative Science and Compassion-Based Ethics (colloquially, the Compassion Center), is one of the first research-based programs to study the physiological, psychological, and behavioral outcomes of compassion training on its participants. It is one of the most researched compassion training programs to date, showing a number of measurable benefits for participants' wellbeing.

A growing body of research in the field of compassion science links compassion training to participants' greater resilience and wellbeing. Studies have suggested that compassion training not only lowers stress hormones and strengthens immune response, but also decreases rumination, activates pleasure circuits in the brain, increases self-reported happiness, creates more optimistic and supportive communication styles, and serves as an antidote to burnout.

In 2004, CBCT was developed by Professor Lobsang Tenzin Negi, bringing together complementary tools from the Indo-Tibetan Buddhist tradition and the emerging science of emotions from psychology and biology, to develop an educational program that contributes to human flourishing. Professor Negi devised CBCT in response to a plea from an undergraduate student at Emory University who saw unmet needs in the mental health crisis faced by her campus community. When taking a course taught by Professor Negi, she found that the practices he presented, on cultivating resilience, self-compassion, and enhancing a sense of belonging and warm-hearted connection to others, could be just what her fellow students needed. Her encouragement led Professor Negi to develop CBCT as a secular program that walks participants through a set of contemplative practices that helps participants establish and cultivate a readily accessible sense of safety, greater self-awareness and emotional pliability, and increased compassion for the self and others.

CBCT Research Outcomes

Significant decreases in:

- stress biomarkers and inflammatory response[1]
- depression[2]
- loneliness[3]
- PTSD symptoms[4]

Significant increases in:

- hopefulness[5]
- compassion and related neural activity[6]
- empathy and related neural activity[7]
- self-compassion[8]

For published research on the above outcomes, visit *compassion.emory.edu*.

26
Countries Represented by Teachers

15
Languages

300+
Certified Teachers

15
Certified Senior Teachers

6,000+
Full Course Participants

15
Introduced to CBCT

As of 2024, CBCT has certified over 300 CBCT teachers from 26 countries, teaching CBCT in 15 languages. CBCT has been offered to over 6000 participants from diverse populations in research settings and to the general public via courses at Emory University. The training has had a transformative impact on educators, healthcare providers, spiritual health practitioners, military veterans with post-traumatic stress disorder (PTSD), adolescents in foster care and in psychiatric hospitals, parents of children with autism, transgender youth and their parents, breast cancer survivors, hospital chaplains, and many others.

How Does CBCT Stand Out from Other Programs?

▶ CBCT holds the distinction of being one of the longest-running and most studied compassion protocols of its kind.

▶ CBCT is linked to improvements in health and wellbeing across studies.

▶ Rather than a one-size-fits-all approach, CBCT has been tailored to various sectors, including education, healthcare, business, and for mental health practitioners, by experts in their respective fields—with impressive results.

▶ CBCT forms the cornerstone of a strategic global initiative, the Compassion Shift®, which aims to advance a global culture of compassion.

CBCT for Mental Health

In 2024, Emory's Compassion Center launched this uniquely tailored program—CBCT for Mental Health—for those who work with individuals experiencing mental health struggles or symptomatology. Practitioners certified in CBCT for Mental Health are able to offer the full course to their clients, providing them with additional practices and tools to foster their growth.

Individuals experiencing mental health distress often feel isolated in their struggles. They suffer alone, convinced that it would be too much of a burden to discuss, share, or bother others with their troubles. Through CBCT for Mental Health, participants can develop skills to improve individual functioning and build interpersonal connections to alleviate feelings of isolation and hopelessness. When facing mental health challenges, it is common to engage in impulsive or maladaptive behaviors as a way to cope with emotions. CBCT with Mental Health offers strategies to help individuals pause and evaluate the potential consequences of their actions, leading to more thoughtful and constructive choices. Participants can engage in daily practices that allow for the blossoming and growth of self-compassion and the understanding that they cannot control all areas of their lives, which evolves into a greater awareness of how others are just like them and also deserve compassion and freedom from suffering. As a result, CBCT for Mental Health fosters greater emotional stability, personal growth, and connection which are essential for mental health and wellbeing.

CBCT for Mental Health is intended as a supplementary practice to any therapeutic regimen. While CBCT is the most researched compassion training program of its kind, it is not currently identified as an evidence-based practice. It is important to explore the symptomatology and treatment modalities identified as effective in addressing the mental health needs of your intended population to determine how CBCT for Mental Health may serve as a secondary resource to this primary work. For example, a person who is struggling with addiction may benefit from CBCT for Mental Health, but their primary

Note: *Throughout this manual, the word "client" is used to refer to individuals who are actively receiving counseling or care from a licensed mental health practitioner. We want to uplift language that indicates the level of service and care provided to others.*

Learn More about CBCT for Mental Health

Training Compassion for Mental Health: The Official Guide to CBCT® for Mental Health (2025).

Compassion U™, the digital learning platform for all CBCT courses. For more information about the CBCT program, courses, and how to bring it to your organization, please visit: *compassionu.app*

treatment function would be some form of substance-use disorder treatment program.

CBCT for Mental Health was tailored by licensed practitioners to be sensitive to the impact of trauma on the body and mind. It was designed to equip clients with tools to navigate the ups and downs of daily life and better manage mental health struggles and symptomatology. With the recognition that internally reflective processes and meditative practices may be more challenging for individuals with moderate to severe mental health needs, **CBCT for Mental Health must be taught by a certified CBCT teacher who is also a licensed clinical mental health practitioner.**

"As a longtime teacher of CBCT and a former therapist, serving many different populations in both capacities, it is so meaningful to witness the insights and changes that participants make as they connect more deeply with the practices of recognizing moments of nurturance and self-compassion in CBCT. Often, I've noticed an initial hesitation, or 'this might work for others, but not sure if it will for me' share at the beginning, and as the course unfolds, with the variety of practice options that CBCT encourages participants to engage with, and the development of community and trust among participants, the moments of care and connection received become visible. The insight of how self-criticism begins to shift to an understanding of one's natural vulnerabilities and inability to control so many circumstances in our lives is powerful. The 'aha' moments that lead to an outward expression of relief (and sometimes joy), as a negative perception of self shifts to one that is much more accepting and kind, are a powerful gift of the practice that participants will sometimes want to attribute to us, as their guides. But it's not us, it is them—their commitment to their practice and the openness and curiosity they bring to explore their own experience."

— CBCT TEACHER AND THERAPIST

Complementary Treatment Modalities for CBCT for Mental Health

As research involving CBCT continues and the work toward attaining evidence-based practice status is underway, it is also helpful to consider how CBCT for Mental Health may align with the ongoing therapeutic programming utilized within an organization or practice. Complementary treatment modalities provide a comprehensive and flexible framework for addressing the individuals' diverse needs. Cognitive Behavioral Therapy helps clients identify and challenge negative thought patterns, promoting healthier behaviors and emotional regulation. Dialectical Behavioral Therapy, with its focus on emotional regulation, distress tolerance, and interpersonal effectiveness, benefits individuals with intense emotional reactions or complex trauma. Trauma-Informed Care, meanwhile, ensures that all interventions are delivered in a way that prioritizes safety, trust, and empowerment, fostering an environment where clients feel supported throughout their healing process. By integrating CBCT for Mental Health alongside these modalities, organizations can offer a holistic, client-centered approach that addresses the underlying causes of mental health challenges while promoting lasting recovery and resilience.

Cognitive Behavioral Therapy (CBT)

- CBT is a well-known and frequently utilized evidence-based treatment modality, shown to be effective in treating depression, anxiety, substance use disorders, PTSD, eating disorders, and many other mental health disorders.[9]

- The practice is focused on identifying and exploring distressing and recurring thoughts and feelings or problematic behaviors. The focus then shifts to challenging and shaping the thoughts, core beliefs, and behaviors to be more based in reality.

- CBT commonly uses critical thinking, reasoning, and rationality to question assumptions and examine challenges and needs from a more logical point of view.

- CBT can be administered within individual, relationship, or group treatment settings, virtually or in-person. An affirming and collaborative partnership with a treatment provider is encouraged.[10]

Dialectical Behavioral Therapy (DBT)

- DBT is an evidence-based psychotherapy utilized to treat a wide range of mental health conditions, including borderline personality disorder, self-harm, suicidal behavior, PTSD, substance use disorder, eating disorders, depression, and anxiety.

- There are four primary skill sets within treatment (mindfulness, acceptance and distress tolerance, emotional regulation, and interpersonal effectiveness), which are developed within weekly individual therapy, skills development–focused group therapy, and crisis coaching and response. Additionally, there are therapist consultation teams for providers.[11]

- The dialectic component of DBT is the intention to address opposite ideas or beliefs, recognizing that there are things an individual cannot change and accepting the things that are within the individual's control, while working toward a more meaningful and satisfactory life.[12]

Trauma-Informed Care (TIC)

- TIC is a comprehensive, evidence-based approach that recognizes the pervasive effects of trauma on individuals and prioritizes their safety, trust, and empowerment. By incorporating principles such as safety, transparency, choice, collaboration, cultural sensitivity, and an understanding of trauma's impact on the brain and body, TIC creates an environment that promotes healing and recovery.[13]

- Recognizing trauma and its long-term consequences as a serious public health crisis is critical, as its impact extends beyond individual health to affect communities and society as a whole. This elevates the significance of integrating trauma-informed practices into care and organizational culture.

- TIC is effective in treating a wide range of mental health disorders that are either directly caused by trauma or exacerbated by traumatic experiences, including PTSD, complex PTSD, anxiety, depression, borderline personality disorder, substance use disorders, eating disorders, and complicated grief.[14]

Compassion-Focused Therapy (CFT)[15]

- Compassion-focused therapy developed from the evolution of the motivational, emotional, behavioral, and cognitive competencies necessary for the higher social functions of noticing and responding to the suffering of others and ourselves.

- It is based on the premise that feelings related to wellbeing and compassion depend upon three emotional regulatory systems: a threat system focused on safety seeking, a drive system focused on resource identification and development, and a soothing system focused on self-regulation and safety.

- CFT was developed as a psychotherapy to help individuals struggling with shame and self-criticism in response to adverse experiences. Internal criticism and self-deprecation are addressed as disruptive threat systems to be attended to through the exploration of painful memories or experiences, and to allow oneself to feel grief and compassion for one's own experience and emotions.

- Through meta-analysis, it has been found to improve levels of self-reassurance and reduce the fear of self-compassion, although additional study is necessary to determine the delivery format that is most efficacious in reducing clinical symptomatology.[16]

Note: *CBCT takes a unique yet complementary approach to CFT, as it was designed to promote resilience, self-compassion, meaningful connections, and flourishing in both clients and providers.*

Meeting the Needs of Mental Health Providers to Engage Compassionate Care

Treating and caring for individuals with mental health needs is an incredibly fulfilling and meaningful role, and it can often be stressful and taxing. Practitioners must have their own coping mechanisms and support systems in place to continue to provide effective and compassionate care. Mental health trends and data indicate that not only are individuals of all ages struggling, but providers' wellbeing and capacity to treat and respond to those with mental health needs have also been declining. It is necessary to examine the areas in which mental health providers are struggling in order to establish systems and practices that ensure mental health providers also receive the care they need.

The Rising Mental Health Crisis

- 1 in 5 US adults experience mental illness each year.[17]

- 1 in 20 US adults experience serious mental illness each year.[18]

- Over the course of a lifetime, about 50 percent of individuals will develop at least one of mental disorder.[19]

- As a global trend, the percentage of young adults aged 18–24 who have mental health distress or are struggling was 3–5 times higher than older adults in the 55–64 age group.

- The lifetime prevalence for any mental disorder is roughly 28–29 percent.[20]

- Younger adults report increasingly higher rates of family instability, conflict, and lack of love and emotional warmth during childhood, despite growing rates of material support by their parents.[21]

- In 2022, 46 percent of health workers reported feeling burned out often or very often, compared with 32 percent in 2018.[22]

- Overall, 44.2 percent of health workers reported being somewhat likely or very likely to look for a new job in 2022.[23]

Provider burnout, secondary traumatic stress, and situations that may blur ethical considerations pose significant risk to the wellbeing of mental health professionals and the quality of care they provide. Responding to mental health needs, experiencing vicarious trauma, and facing a lack of community or cultural support can greatly reduce providers' wellbeing. Mental health providers may experience emotional exhaustion, empathic distress, and a sense of detachment from their work due to the rising mental health crisis and intense emotional demands of supporting clients through trauma and struggles with symptoms. This can lead to a decreased capacity for compassion and increased feelings of ineffectiveness, ultimately affecting the quality of client care. Attuning to and caring for the needs of mental health providers is a critical component of compassionate mental health care. By addressing the needs of providers, we ensure that they can continue to offer the highest quality of care, maintain their wellbeing, and contribute to the overall success of the therapeutic process.

CBCT can work to benefit both the client and the practitioner. While CBCT has been tailored for the client through this CBCT for Mental Health program, CBCT is offered in a variety of forms - for the general public, for healthcare providers, for educators, and for business and leadership professionals. It is encouraged for practitioners offering CBCT for Mental Health to their clients to engage in a personal practice as well. The practitioner's personal practice leads to subtle (and sometimes not-so-subtle) changes in their emotional and social intelligence. The practices are designed to naturally shift small interactions—use of language, tone of voice, or gestures—that can make a world of difference to the individuals they serve and care for. These subtle gestures, and the way in which they engage, encourage, and prompt growth and exploration for their clients within CBCT, can enhance trust and confidence within the provider–client relationship. And as mental health providers reinforce these practices for their clients, they are simultaneously improving their own wellbeing and confidence in their practice.

A Glossary of Key Issues Facing Providers

Provider burnout	syndrome resulting from chronic workplace stress that has not been managed. Characterized by three dimensions: sustained feelings of exhaustion; increased mental distance from or feelings of cynicism related to one's job; and professional inefficacy.[24]
Empathic distress	the strongly felt or experienced embodiment of another person's distress in respons to their suffering, which results in an individual's attempt to disengage from a situation in order to avoid additional negative feelings.[25]
Moral injury	the psychological, spiritual, or ethical violation of an individual's moral beliefs or conscience when they are exposed to or fail to act in a traumatic or highly stressful situation.[26]
Secondary traumatic stress:	the emotional distress an individual experiences after hearing about or witnessing trauma experienced by another person, which can often take an emotional toll after listening to traumatic stories for an extended period of time.[27]
Challenges of ethics and integrity	the gray area of client care in response to challenges in practice, including disclosure, advancements in technology, reporting concerns, and other ambiguous and significant decision-making situations.

The Research behind the Practice

CBCT is an effective, research-based program that has been shown to improve many mental health symptoms and challenges. Treating the mental health needs of clients in any setting means ensuring that treatment modalities are aligned with and effective in the population served. When exploring the implementation of CBCT for Mental Health as a component of treatment, the symptomology and diagnostics of the clients in your practice or program should be among the highest considerations. There has already been considerable research conducted on the efficacy of CBCT and its ability to improve specific mental health and wellbeing outcomes.

What follows are two case studies outlining the application of CBCT and its outcomes in two specific populations.

CBCT for Patients and Their Partners

Dr. Corina Aguilar-Raab has developed a pioneering research program aimed at enhancing the treatment of depression through the integration of CBCT. Her research is organized under the name SIDE study (Social Interaction in Depression Enhancement), a randomized controlled trial that uniquely incorporates both the depressed patient and their romantic partner into the therapeutic process.[28] The rationale behind this approach is grounded in evidence that depression not only affects the individual but also impairs relationship quality and the health of their partner, thereby diminishing the benefits of positive social interactions.

The adapted intervention, known as CBCT for Couples (CBCT-fC), is a 10-week program designed to cultivate compassion, emotional regulation, and empathy within the dyad. Participants engage in guided meditation practices and reflective exercises that aim to shift cognitive patterns and foster a deeper sense of connection and mutual support. The study employs a comprehensive set of measures, including psychological assessments, eye-tracking during social interactions, and biological markers, such as cortisol and inflammatory cytokines, to evaluate the impact of the training on both mental health and physiological stress responses.

This research is notable for its biopsychosocial approach, combining contemplative science with clinical psychology and psychobiology. By involving both partners in the intervention, the program seeks not only to alleviate depressive symptoms but also to strengthen the couple's relational dynamics, thereby creating a more supportive environment for recovery. The intervention was effective in decreasing current depressive symptomatology and increasing mindfulness and self-compassion. Participants also reported finding meaning and other emotional benefits from engaging in the practice between sessions.

This innovative model holds promise for expanding the scope of compassion-based therapies and underscores the importance of relational context in mental health treatment.

This work has inspired other researchers to consider dyadic offerings in other applications—for example, for the improvement of psychological symptoms following successful solid-tumor cancer treatments. Dr. Thaddeus Pace of the University of Arizona, who has researched CBCT with breast cancer survivors for many years, is currently in the midst of a five-year trial funded by the US National Institute of Health that offers CBCT remotely (by video conference) to recovered patients and their supportive partners, known as the SUPORT project. This study is scheduled to be completed in 2027. Preliminary reports confirm the feasibility of the approach and provide anecdotal evidence of positive outcomes.

CBCT for Veterans with PTSD

CBCT-Veteran was developed to explore the potential of CBCT as a complementary intervention for veterans suffering from PTSD. Recognizing that many veterans either do not engage with or do not fully benefit from traditional PTSD treatments, researchers sought to adapt CBCT to better align with military culture and the specific psychological needs of this population. The program was designed to cultivate compassion for the self and others, enhance emotional regulation, and reduce the symptoms of trauma-related distress.

Working through the VA San Diego Healthcare System and the University of California, San Diego, Dr. Ariel Lang and Dr. Pollyanna Casmar collaborated with Dr. Lobsang Tenzin Negi and Timothy Harrison of the Emory Compassion Center on the development and evaluation of CBCT-Veteran. Funded by a series of grants from the National Institute

"As teachers, our capacities to 'be with' and not need to 'fix' or change participants are so crucial to this transformation. In the 'being with,' I always find that I am learning so much from the courage and resilience of participants who take up CBCT practice in their lives, and I am always moved by the depth of compassion that emerges in the community as the course unfolds with a group."

— CBCT-CERTIFIED TEACHER AND THERAPIST

of Mental Health, the team led a series of studies that iteratively refined the CBCT protocol for veterans. Their work included both non-randomized and randomized trials, as well as telehealth adaptations. The team used quantitative and qualitative feedback from participants to tailor the language, pacing, and content of the sessions, ensuring the material was digestible and relevant to veterans' lived experiences.

Initial research outcomes were promising. In a non-randomized study involving 36 veterans, participation in CBCT-Veteran was associated with significant reductions in PTSD and depression symptoms, with effect sizes suggesting meaningful clinical improvement.[29] A follow-up study emphasized the importance of home meditation practice, showing that veterans who engaged more consistently in home practice experienced greater improvements in depression, negative affect, and positive affect.[30] These findings highlight both the feasibility and therapeutic potential of CBCT for this population, especially when supported by regular practice. Despite these encouraging results, the researchers noted that improvements in positive emotion and social connectedness were less consistent, suggesting areas for further refinement.

The research team as well as the therapists who were trained as CBCT teachers to offer CBCT-Veteran feel that this program represents a significant step forward in integrating contemplative science with trauma recovery, offering a compassionate, culturally sensitive alternative for veterans who may not respond to conventional therapies.

CBCT Studies: Results and Impact

The following highlights the impact of CBCT training on symptoms studied across CBCT research. For a more inclusive list of CBCT research, please visit *compassion.emory.edu*.

Exploration examined whether a 6-week CBCT intervention would improve psychosocial functioning among adolescents in foster care.[31]

Practice frequency was associated with **increased hopefulness** and a trend for a **decrease in generalized anxiety**. Qualitative results indicated that participants found CBCT useful for dealing with daily stressors.

Exploration of CBCT's effects on breast cancer survivors in an 8-week group and then a 4-week booster group format to examine symptom change, including depression, intrusive thoughts, perceived stress, fear of cancer recurrence, fatigue/vitality, loneliness, and quality of life.[32]

Suggestions of **significant improvements in depression, avoidance of intrusive thoughts, functional impairment associated with fear of recurrence, mindfulness, and vitality/fatigue.** At follow-up, **less perceived stress** and **higher mindfulness** were also significant in the CBCT group.

Exploration of CBCT's efficacy in altering compassion, loneliness, stress, depression, and general functioning, while examining who benefited most from compassion meditation.[33]

Participants found an **increase in compassion** and a **decrease in loneliness and depression**.

Comparison of the effectiveness of CBCT group treatment to a support group in reducing depressive symptoms and suicidal ideation, and increasing self-compassion and mindfulness in low-income African Americans who had attempted suicide.[34]

Participants saw **improvements in levels of self-compassion and mindfulness**, with a **reduction of depression and suicidal ideation** and **improved psychological functioning.**

Exploration of CBCT-CM (Compassion Meditation) practiced by veterans who have PTSD; focused on the veterans' ability to stabilize attention, develop present-moment awareness, and foster compassion through weekly measures of PTSD, depressive symptoms, and positive and negative emotions.[35]

Reductions in overall PTSD-symptom severity: reexperiencing, hyperarousal, and negative alterations in cognition, as well as **reductions in depressive symptoms**

Examination of CBCT practiced by people with HIV to determine if it could reduce inflammation and psychological stress in individuals living with HIV who fail to fully restore CD4+ T-cell counts.[36]

A significant association between CBCT practice time engagement and **fold-reduction in IL-6 and TNF-levels**. Practice was associated with **improvements in general wellbeing, along with HIV disease acceptance and other benefits. Fewer instances of virologic failure** were observed for those in the CBCT arm compared to controls.

Different sex couples, where the female partner had depression, explored whether CBCT was more effective than treatment as usual in reducing depressive symptoms; enhancing contemplative qualities such as mindfulness and self-compassion; increasing perceived relationship quality and perceived social support within the couple; and altering stress responses.[37]

CBCT-fC (CBCT for Couples) was effective in **decreasing current depressive symptomatology and increasing mindfulness and self-compassion**. Participants reported **finding meaning and other emotional benefits** from engaging in the practice between sessions.

CBCT Implementation in Action

Mental health care is provided in outpatient clinics, day programs, residential treatment facilities, substance abuse programming, hospitals, doctors' offices, criminal justice settings, and schools. Providers in each of these settings could include licensed mental health clinicians, chaplains, guidance counselors, peer-to-peer mentors, and other carers. We feel it is important to examine and explore how different organizations have implemented CBCT within their programming to serve individuals with mental health needs. The case studies that follow describe how CBCT was implemented in several different organizations.

Note: *See Appendix A for a sample three-year implementation plan.*

Implementation of CBCT at Hillside, Inc., Atlanta, Georgia

Hillside, Inc. is a mental health treatment provider for adolescents and their families in Atlanta, Georgia. The team at Hillside provides residential psychiatric treatment and an extended day program on their campus, as well as outpatient services throughout the state of Georgia. While the program itself is a DBT-Linehan–certified program, it also offers Theraplay, horticulture therapy, and other trauma-informed treatment modalities. In 2018, its leadership felt that they wanted to bring more compassion to the culture of Hillside, for the benefit of its staff, its patients, and the families served. In 2019, six staff went through the CBCT course and the Teacher Certification program.

"CBCT has helped me so much at my stay here at Hillside. I've learned that I need to respect myself the same as I respect others. I've learned self-compassion and basically how to treat someone the right way."

— HILLSIDE PATIENT

Hillside experienced some turnover in staff during the process, so by the time all teachers were able to achieve certification, there were four teachers fully certified. At the end of 2021, pilot groups were implemented and run on two of the seven cottages on Hillside's campus. Many of the youth served at Hillside have extensive trauma histories, and it was decided to create a space on Hillside's campus just for CBCT and reflective, calming practices. Hillside built a yurt and converted it into a therapeutic meditation space for patients and staff to enjoy.

During the pilot phase, Hillside focused on exploring assessment tools, solidifying data collection, bolstering staff training and engagement, and ensuring that scheduling could support and sustain a new group to be implemented campus-wide. As of January 2024, the CBCT group is offered to each of Hillside's seven cottages, twice weekly, for an hour session each time.

CBCT Implementation at Hillside

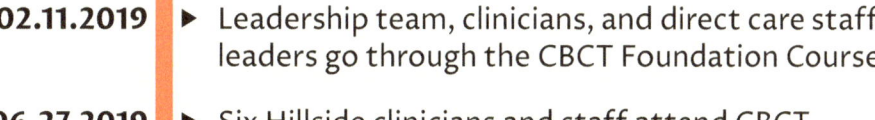

02.11.2019 ▶ Leadership team, clinicians, and direct care staff leaders go through the CBCT Foundation Course

06.27.2019 ▶ Six Hillside clinicians and staff attend CBCT Teacher Certification program

05.2021 ▶ Hillside clinicians and staff who complete CBCT teacher training are officially certified teachers

11.2021 ▶ Twice weekly CBCT groups are implemented on two cottages

08.22.2022 ▶ Hillside teachers join the Compassion Shift initiative

01.15.2024 ▶ CBCT groups are implemented campus wide at Hillside

Hillside's 2023 standardized outcome measures showed patient functioning and wellbeing improved in many ways, including:

- ✎ Overall improvement in their ability to regulate their negative emotions

- ✎ Increase in non-judgmental and non-reactive attitudes to negative thoughts and feelings

- ✎ Overall improvement in their ability to handle uncomfortable emotional experiences

- ✎ Increased ability to regulate their emotions and reactions to changes in their moods

"As a therapist and CBCT-certified teacher, the practices have intrinsically changed me. I feel like I have the tools to create more grounded and reflective spaces in my own life. My ability to notice, pause, breathe, and reflect before responding or reacting has been greatly improved, and thus improves my ability to care for and be present for my clients and their families. I am so grateful to have had the opportunity to learn from some amazing teachers and pass that knowledge on to my students."

— Hillside staff member, therapist, and certified CBCT teacher

Improvements in wellbeing were also captured in feedback from CBCT participants that emphasized the positive difference they feel in their lives. Implementing CBCT at Hillside has had a powerful impact on both patients and staff and continues to contribute to a greater culture of compassion across the organization.

"What we didn't expect, but were really happy to see, was how the staff who would bring clients to groups would also participate in the meditations and the group discussions, and would spend time processing through a harder lesson with some of our clients who needed extra time to internalize a concept. The staff shared how much they enjoyed being able to take some quiet and reflective time out of their generally chaotic and fast-paced days in the CBCT for Mental Health group. We got to see direct-care staff stepping up as leaders and building stronger bonds of connection with our residents."

— HILLSIDE STAFF MEMBER, therapist, and certified CBCT teacher

Implementation of CBCT in Healthcare Education

CBCT for Mental Health was designed with the intention that participants move through the course with a licensed mental health practitioner. CBCT for Healthcare Providers is another tailored program intended for those who identify as healthcare providers (e.g., nurses, physicians, physical therapists, hospital chaplains, clinical psychologists, etc.).

In some cases, mental health professionals looking to take CBCT may choose the CBCT for Healthcare Providers version of the course, which primarily tailors the material to clinical experiences. For mental health professionals whose work mostly falls outside of clinical experience, we recommend they take the general CBCT course.

Before the launch of CBCT for Healthcare Providers, CBCT had already been integrated into several healthcare systems. Two examples are described here:

Emory School of Medicine: In 2014, the leaders of the Emory School of Medicine invited Professor Negi, PhD to teach a comprehensive CBCT course to 20 of the top school leaders, including Dean Christian Larsen, MD. From this, Dean Larsen and other leaders—including Executive Dean of Education William J. Eley, MD, and Associate Dean of Students Ira Schwartz, MD—became convinced that CBCT could serve as an antidote to a number of the common struggles that plague physicians and seem to begin during their medical training, including depersonalization, depression, suicidality, and anxiety.

The interest that this generated led to Dean Larsen's funding of a randomized control trial, led by veteran CBCT researcher and medical anthropologist, Jennifer Mascaro, PhD, that tailored CBCT for second-year medical students and showed a significant increase in compassion and decreases in loneliness, sleep disturbances, and depression symptoms. For more than 10 years now, Emory's Compassion Center has successfully taught CBCT to hundreds of Emory physicians and physicians-in-training, as well as to genetic counselors, physical therapists, nurses, and physician's assistants, via this partnership.

Emory Spiritual Health: In 2016, another partnership bloomed with Emory Healthcare—this time, with the Department of Spiritual Health, which oversees the hospital chaplains and houses one of the largest hospital-chaplaincy training programs in the United States. The leadership in Spiritual Health, especially Executive Director George Grant, PhD, and Director of Education Maureen Shelton, MDiv, had been searching for a training program that would address the emerging and changing needs for hospital chaplains—especially the real need to serve an increasingly diverse population of patients and staff who bring with them a widening variety of beliefs and traditions. They found CBCT's approach promising from the start, thanks to its emphasis on values and ethics and its alignment with many people's understanding of spirituality, while also respecting the beliefs of all major faith traditions.

At first, CBCT was folded into chaplaincy education, but soon the chaplains began to report using their CBCT practices to support active patient and staff encounters. From these insights, CCSH™ (Compassion-Centered Spiritual Health) was established and soon evolved into a formal training curriculum that builds on CBCT to bolster the wellbeing, resilience, and compassion of healthcare patients and staff. This generative collaboration between Emory University's Spiritual Health at the Woodruff Health Sciences Center and Emory's Compassion Center augments spiritual health education and best practices with CBCT. CCSH interventions are delivered by spiritual care professionals trained in both CBCT and ACPE: The Standard in Spiritual Care and Education. Emory now trains chaplains internationally and certifies them as CCSH Registered Clinicians. See *ccsh.emory.edu* for more information.

Implementation Process

A cohesive plan for implementing CBCT for Mental Health within a practice or organization goes far beyond attending a few sessions or just going through the training. Implementation involves exploring how to intentionally integrate a new practice and philosophical approach to care, while balancing the logistics of changing procedures and programming in a meaningful and sustainable way.

CBCT for Mental Health aims to develop competencies of resilience, awareness, discernment, and compassion to strengthen wellbeing and develop a culture of care and compassion in individuals with mental

The Four Components
of CBCT for Mental Health Implementation

1		**Establish Leadership and Vision**	Lay the groundwork for the implementation of CBCT for Mental Health.
2		**Cultivate Collaborative Engagement**	Introduce CBCT for Mental Health to the practice or organization to create buy-in and offer opportunities to engage staff in CBCT for Mental Health.
3		**Implement the Training**	Plan, deliver, and assess the CBCT for Mental Health training.
4		**Support Ongoing Integration**	Sustain, develop, and continuously integrate CBCT for Mental Health.

health needs. Depending on the practice or organizational setting, the implementation process may have different timelines, identified outcomes, funding concerns, and challenges or barriers to sustainability.

Given the limited resources mental health and nonprofit systems have to meet the many (behavioral, academic, social–emotional, psychological, etc.) needs of clients and their families, the investment of time, resources, and money into staff wellbeing can seem less of a priority. However, it is widely accepted across multiple research studies that the efficacy of a clinician and the clinician's relationship with the client contribute significantly to the client's mental health and wellbeing.[38] Investing in the wellbeing of providers and clinicians alike is investing in the wellbeing of clients and all stakeholders.

When implementing and sustaining CBCT for Mental Health, there are several components to consider. This section illustrates various options for how practitioners and organizations can approach these components to implement CBCT into their practices and systems at a larger scale.

Component 1
Establish Leadership and Vision

 Establish Leadership Buy-in and Roles

To generate interest in shifting the organization's culture toward compassion, it is important to cultivate buy-in and investment from leadership. Exploration of stakeholders and community members is not only critical for the longevity of the practice, but it can also aid in funding opportunities.

At the beginning of the implementation process, the project might be spearheaded by one or two individuals (a clinician, staff member, supervisor, administrator, department head, manager, director, etc.) who are interested in integrating CBCT into their program, or it may be a group of individuals eager to engage in this work. These interested parties may form the beginnings of the CBCT for Mental Health committee. This committee is more formally established and expanded in Component 2.

While any clinician or staff member may drive the implementation process, gaining leadership buy-in and support will be critical for successful implementation and ongoing program maintenance. The leadership supporting CBCT implementation may change and grow as CBCT moves further into implementation and sustainability practices.

Understanding the Role of Leadership

The motivation and efforts of organizational leadership are critical to successfully integrating CBCT competencies and supporting staff through challenges that may arise. Through authentic modeling and integration of CBCT principles, a leader can support the implementation of CBCT, and its many practices can become skillfully woven into the fabric of a client-serving, mental health, and compassion-focused mission.

Leadership should also consider which stakeholders can support the shift toward a more compassionate organizational culture, and what tangible support they could receive, such as community or board engagement, funding resources, or contributions from donors. Depending on the organization, stakeholders could consist of other nonprofit or for-profit corporations, board members, community members, donors, parents or relatives of clients, or other groups. Starting conversations with these stakeholders early helps to set the foundation for this work to succeed.

Leadership Engagement and Authentic Modeling

Framing CBCT for Mental Health as a shared responsibility fosters a non-hierarchical approach and creates a mutually beneficial investment for wellbeing and organizational cohesion. As CBCT is implemented organization-wide and staff engage with its philosophies and tenets, leaders must actively demonstrate authentic leadership by modeling the roles and behaviors they expect from others. This includes consistently practicing CBCT principles, integrating them into daily interactions, and setting clear examples for staff to follow. The following practices will help leaders embed CBCT into the organizational culture and drive successful implementation:

Authentic Modeling	• Actively engaging and being present in training and staff discussions • Sharing or showing ways in which CBCT for Mental Health skills have been applied to your daily life and interactions
Integrating CBCT for Mental Health Practices	• Incorporating practical applications into meetings, communications, and programmatic routines • Establishing consistent and clear messaging of CBCT concepts and topics
Celebrating and Uplifting	• Acknowledging accomplishments, engagement, and milestones for clients, groups, and staff • Speaking about and highlighting the benefits of implementation and engagement
Establishing Systems and Structures	• Supporting the CBCT committee that can guide and drive the work of implementation • Acquiring the needed resources and support to be able to provide time and space for staff workshops, training, and practice

 ## Determine Goals and Vision

Determining the goals and vision of implementing CBCT for Mental Health in an organization or program sets the foundation for this work. The following questions should be considered to gain clarity about the desired outcomes before formally engaging in implementation. If there is a group involved in this early phase of implementation, a meeting should be held to discuss these points and agree upon goals and direction, and put together a brief, program-specific vision and mission.

Guiding Questions — Determine Goals and Vision

How will CBCT for Mental Health improve our existing programming?

How does CBCT for Mental Health differ from other programs or initiatives, and how does it stand out?

What outcomes do we hope to see in our client population to justify implementing a new program?

Are there other areas of patient flow or need that CBCT Mental Health may impact?

How does CBCT for Mental Health align with our current mission and vision?

 ## Assess Needs and Readiness

Determining the organization's readiness for CBCT implementation is important because of the variety of mental health organizational systems and their needs. The following questions can help to determine the current capacity for sustainability and conditions for implementation, including capacity, resources, assets, and needs, as well as any anticipated barriers or areas of challenge. This process builds on the vision and goal-setting reflection to support implementation.

Guiding Questions — Assess Needs and Readiness

How do we expect announcing the implementation of CBCT to be received? Do we know if our staff are experiencing new-initiative fatigue?

Are there ongoing initiatives and projects that staff are participating in concurrently? Are we planning any other large-scale, organization-wide developments over the next two to three years?

Is there a specific department CBCT for Mental Health would align with and could live within?

Describe the overall staff morale. What considerations need to be made to support, improve, and/or sustain the current culture and climate?

What is already in place (wellness programming, healthcare initiatives, team-building activities, staff appreciation events, etc.) that we can build upon and use to support this work?

What is the composition of our staff? Do we have primarily experienced, long-term staffing, or are we experiencing challenges with staff turnover?

Who are the primary stakeholders who could support the implementation work?

Do staff have professional development time available? What will staffing look like for teacher training, certification, and ongoing learning?

What financial, human, and programmatic resources are available to plan and support training and implementation?

What do our staff have the capacity to commit to? What will be needed to sustain the work?

Cultivate Collaborative Engagement

2	Cultivate Collaborative Engagement		
	Introduce CBCT for Mental Health to the practice or organization to create buy-in and offer opportunities to engage staff in CBCT for Mental Health		Offer an Orientation Session
			Form a CBCT for Mental Health Committee
		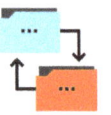	Develop an Outreach and Communication Plan
			Engage Staff in CBCT
			Identify Funding and Resources

 ## Offer an Orientation Session

The orientation session aims to introduce CBCT for Mental Health to a group that can serve as the program's early adopters and/or individuals who would be interested in being part of the planning process. There may be one large session for the whole staff or multiple sessions for different groups within the community.

This one- to two-hour orientation session is designed to provide basic knowledge about and understanding of the CBCT for Mental Health program, its design, and how it can be implemented. This session covers its framework and history, its benefits for mental health providers, its approach to cultivating resilience and wellbeing, and the science that supports it. The orientation is also designed to help participants better understand how CBCT for Mental Health implementation can meet

Orientation Session Content

An Overview of CBCT for Mental Health (~15 min)

This section will briefly outline the framework and background of CBCT, its benefits for participants, its approach to cultivating resilience and wellbeing, and the science that supports it.

Note: *For a more in-depth overview that includes reflective and interactive practices, a certified CBCT teacher is required to facilitate. See "Introductory Offerings" on page 32 for more information.*

The Implementation Process (~30 min)

This section goes over the goals of and options for implementation, possible next steps, and community engagement opportunities. When describing this process, the facilitator can consider the following:

- Articulate a clear alignment to existing organizational vision and strategy.
- Articulate a clear rationale for choosing to implement CBCT.
- Be authentic about their personal investment in CBCT.
- Make connections between CBCT and complementary treatment modalities.
- Highlight how CBCT stands out and what makes CBCT different. Discuss the challenges and opportunities that may arise from this work.
- Acknowledge, if appropriate, the possibility of change fatigue in the organization.

Discussion, Collaboration, and Further Communication (~15 min)

Lastly, the facilitator should field questions and hear from individuals in the session about ideas, areas for further consideration, and any concerns raised. In preparation for this discussion, the facilitator will lead the group in the co-creation of guiding principles that will make them feel safe, heard, not judged, etc.

The content and outcomes of the orientation session can be made available to the whole organization via communication channels, as appropriate.

the needs of the organization or program. When introducing CBCT for Mental Health to staff, it is important to communicate a thoughtful and carefully crafted message that is aligned with the organization's values and culture—or a message that represents the culture shift the organization hopes to move toward.

 ## Form a CBCT for Mental Health Committee

Once CBCT for Mental Health is introduced through the orientation session, different members of the organization may become interested in engaging in the implementation work. This is a great opportunity to invite colleagues and staff from different disciplines to join the CBCT committee.

Developing and maintaining a CBCT committee helps the implementation process to be inclusive. It creates opportunities for members of the organization at different levels of leadership and from different disciplines to be involved in the implementation and feel a sense of ownership over the work.

The make-up of a CBCT committee will vary based on the organization's values, capacity, and interest levels. The composition of the team depends on the organization's size, purpose, and function. It may be beneficial to have someone with decision-making power as an active part of the team.

Committee members can be identified in multiple ways. One of the most important is providing a transparent application process so that all members of the organization feel invited to participate in the process of CBCT review, piloting, and implementation. Focused outreach to key members is beneficial as well.

Suggestions for Forming Your CBCT for Mental Health Committee

- Members for the committee should include select organizational leaders, select stakeholders invested in CBCT programming and compassionate care, and staff completing CBCT Teacher Certification. For information on CBCT Teacher Certification, see page 34.

- Consider who within the organization is critical for CBCT's success and who can be engaged on a consultant-type basis. For example, if you are including data collection or measurement options in assessing CBCT's success, do your performance/ quality improvement team members need to be included in the committee, or can they be engaged as necessary for consultation on the data collection process?

- Regarding leadership's involvement: How engaged does organizational leadership need to be in the day-to-day functioning of the implementation? Who may want to be involved but may not have the time? Is there a staff member that is approved to make financial decisions or programmatic development decisions? Who is most responsible for CBCT programming?

There may be staff whose feedback would be particularly valuable but who do not have time or the capacity to commit to participating fully as a certified teacher or on the committee. There may also be staff members interested in assisting with implementing CBCT or becoming certified teachers but who would struggle to fulfill the responsibilities for their primary roles if they were to add CBCT responsibilities as well. In these instances, the CBCT committee should explore alternative options for involvement. These staff members (e.g., performance-quality improvement staff, direct-care staff, grant writers, and development or finance team members) may be able to stay engaged through consultation or collaboration rather than becoming committee members or certified teachers. The team should be collaborative, with representation from as many stakeholder groups as possible.

 ## Develop an Outreach and Communication Plan

The CBCT committee should develop a communication plan. The purpose of communication related to CBCT for Mental Health is to inform and engage the staff about why CBCT is being implemented, what they can expect from CBCT, and how they can get involved in CBCT.

Looking at ways for all members of the organization to be involved in CBCT's implementation will create a stronger sense of cohesion and engagement through the implementation process.

Communication Plan Goals

- Gaining support from organization employees
- Sparking interest in different stakeholder groups
- Developing relationships to allow for questions and exploration of CBCT
- Sharing information about different CBCT offerings and practices
- Keeping people engaged and excited about CBCT practices and training experiences
- Providing support for initial and ongoing CBCT integration

 ## Engage Staff in CBCT

Engaging staff in CBCT is an essential step in the implementation process. This allows staff to gain a personalized understanding of the program and its benefits before it is offered to clients. It also gives staff an opportunity to begin their own personal practice with CBCT. As was discussed earlier, bringing CBCT to clients, staff, and practitioners is the best way to infuse compassion into the organization and contribute to the wellbeing of all stakeholders. Organizational leadership and the CBCT committee will need to examine which format of CBCT introduction and staff training will most effectively engage staff.

Introductory Offerings

As an introduction to CBCT, many organizations may utilize an all-staff training opportunity to provide a taster session. For those who are not yet ready for the complete training, the team can consider the following options:

Overview of Training Compassion (30 minutes–1.5 hours)

Brief Description: The Overview offered in the Training Compassion course on Compassion U orients participants to the content and practices of the course. This self-guided experience introduces compassion and compassion training, and includes reflective exercises and practices that set a foundation for the course and give a glimpse into the types of experiences that participants will engage in throughout the rest of the course. The Overview is free and available to anyone through Compassion U.

Format: Self-guided on digital e-learning platform, Compassion U

Introduction to CBCT – Seminar (45 minutes–3 hours)

Brief Description: An introduction to CBCT, including a sample practice or two. This training provides an overview of CBCT, including an exploration of the framework and history, its benefits, its approach to cultivating resilience and wellbeing, and the science that supports it.

Format: Live session in person or via videoconference, facilitated by a certified CBCT teacher

A Taste of CBCT – Workshop (4–8 hours)

Brief Description: This workshop exposes participants to the key themes, skills, and insights of the CBCT course, and introduces some of the reflective exercises and informal and formal practices. This workshop provides a taste of the CBCT experience, allowing individuals to begin exploring and strengthening the capacities related to resilience and compassion before diving into the training. This could be done in one long session or broken up into several shorter sessions over multiple days.

Format: Live session(s) in person or via videoconference, facilitated by a certified CBCT teacher

Training Compassion

Participating in the training is the best way for staff and practitioners to become familiar with CBCT and see the personal benefits it can bring. This is especially valuable for practitioners interested in offering this training to future clients. Taking this course in full is a requirement for anyone applying to be part of the CBCT Teacher Certification program.

Training Compassion (16–24 hours)

Brief Description: A deep dive into the eight CBCT modules. Each module introduces new content, reflective exercises, and practices designed to strengthen inner skills and support their application into everyday life.

The Training Compassion course is offered through Compassion U, a user-friendly app that delivers CBCT course content and provides access to instructional videos, activities, practices, and a compassion community, among other resources.

Courses include live sessions with other participants, facilitated by certified CBCT teachers. These live sessions are typically one hour long and occur weekly over nine weeks. Prior to each live session, participants engage in the self-guided content, activities, and practices on Compassion U. For more information on CBCT courses, please visit *compassionu.app*.

Format:

▶ Self-guided on digital e-learning platform, Compassion U (8–16 hours, typically 1.5 hours per week)

▶ Live sessions in person or via videoconference, facilitated by a certified CBCT teacher (9 hours of live sessions, typically 1 hour per week)

CBCT Teacher Certification

The CBCT Teacher Certification program deepens the practice of the participant, increasing their capacity to offer and embed CBCT for Mental Health within mental health-serving systems. One of the best and most sustainable ways to ensure supported and ongoing implementation of CBCT for Mental Health is to provide pathways for interested practitioners to become CBCT-certified teachers. The CBCT Teacher Certification program is designed to provide high-quality teaching of CBCT for research purposes, as well as the general sharing of CBCT skills and content with a wider audience.

A mental health practitioner will need to decide how they will allocate their time to complete teacher certification. Individual clinicians or practitioners should determine what may need to shift or remain flexible within their schedule while going through the teacher certification to allow for more time and energy to be dedicated to the training while not overburdening oneself. Before applying for CBCT Teacher Certification, a practitioner should envision the population they would like to bring CBCT to and confirm it aligns with the other treatment modalities in their practice.

Identify Funding and Resources

Identifying sources of funding from grants, the general budget, the professional development budget, and other sources is essential for engaging in the planning process. An important step in planning and coordinating implementation is identifying the resources and funds needed for initial CBCT training, CBCT Teacher Certification, and/or compensation for staff attending trainings or engaging in CBCT-related duties outside of their official role. Implementing CBCT for

---

Encouraging Staff to Become Certified CBCT Teachers

▶ Offer regular CBCT courses or share information about CBCT courses offered by Emory University through Compassion U. Taking the CBCT course as a participant is a prerequisite for the CBCT Teacher Certification program.

▶ Share the following information about the CBCT Teacher Certification program with staff and leaders interested in implementing CBCT for Mental Health:

- Opportunities / benefits of certification
  - Ability to teach CBCT to members of the organization, clients, and the general public
  - Access to a global compassion community of other certified CBCT teachers
  - Deepened familiarity with the content and practices of CBCT and enhanced personal wellbeing
- Funding/scholarship opportunities available to them (if applicable)
- Certification process details (visit *compassionu.app/teacher-certification* for this information)

Mental Health will include many expenses, with the bulk of the initial expense being the CBCT Teacher Certification. An organization also needs to consider expenses related to office space, utilities, equipment, participant or group supplies, print material, and any other infrastructure development needed to fully integrate CBCT for Mental Health into programming for staff and clients.

Organizations should consider how to cover the cost for clients to gain access to the CBCT for Mental Health course in Compassion U. This might involve using pre-existing programming funds, increasing the cost of services provided for clients, or securing external funding. Additionally, there are costs for evaluating CBCT for Mental Health's effectiveness with clients, including assessment tools, data collection and materials, and staff wages. Contingency funding would be beneficial to cover any unexpected costs, supply needs, or improvement considerations. It is important for an organization's leadership to determine the costs of implementing and sustaining CBCT for Mental Health, and how those expenses weigh into the intended effects for clients and the benefit CBCT for Mental Health will bring to the clients, practitioners, and culture of the organization.

Many organizations are required either by federal, state, or accrediting regulations to maintain an evidence-based treatment approach in order to bill or be reimbursed for services provided. If organizations are implementing CBCT for Mental Health alongside a complementary treatment modality, they should work with their financial and development departments to determine how to best seek payment for services.

Budget Considerations

- Program design
- Staff training and wages
- Technology and software
- Office space updates and decorations
- Print material and supplies for participants
- Surveys or assessment material
- Program maintenance
- Contingency funding

Component 3
Implement the Training

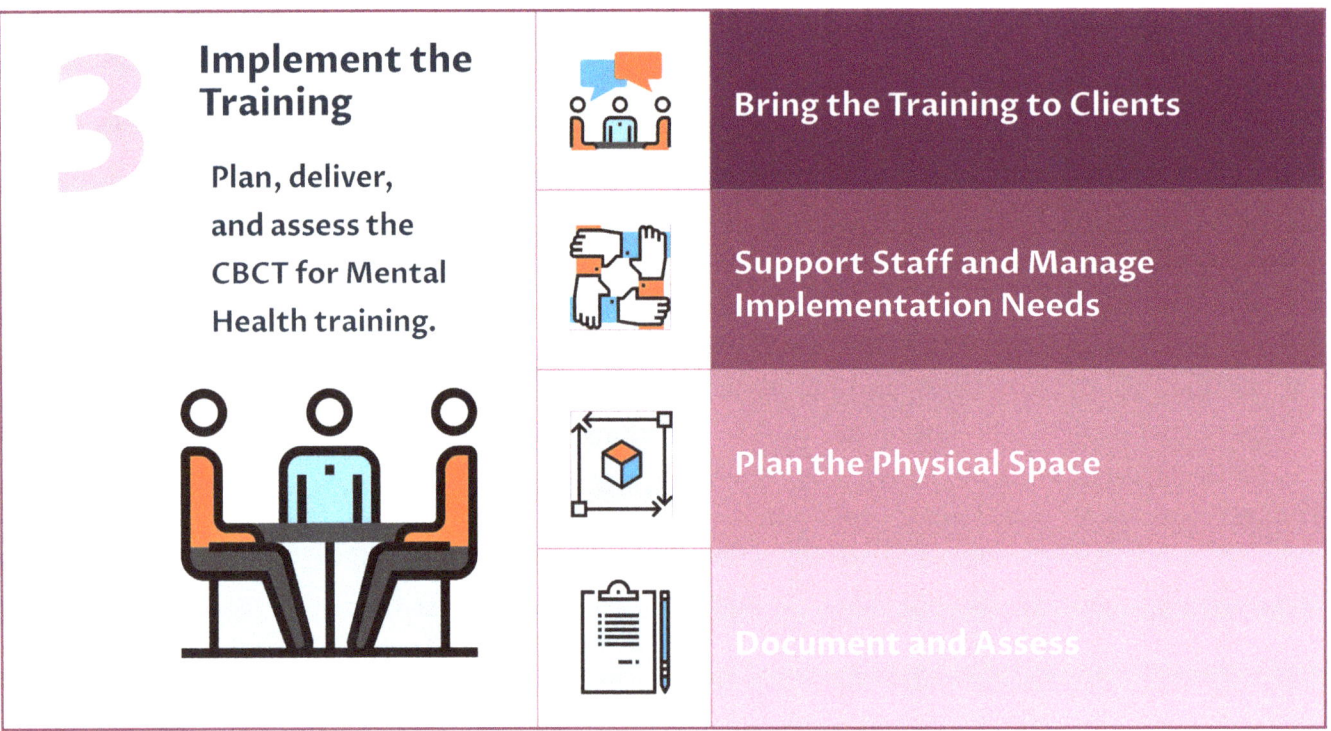

Implement the Training

Plan, deliver, and assess the CBCT for Mental Health training.

	Bring the Training to Clients
	Support Staff and Manage Implementation Needs
	Plan the Physical Space
	Document and Assess

 ## Bring the Training to Clients

CBCT for Mental Health is designed to be delivered to individuals who have mental health symptoms and/or diagnoses, and it must be taught by an Emory University–certified CBCT teacher who is also a licensed clinical mental health practitioner.

CBCT for Mental Health can be implemented across a variety of programmatic structures serving mental health needs. A single organization may incorporate programs that are entirely in person, entirely virtual, or through some hybrid option for varying aspects of care. CBCT for Mental Health has options for organizations and providers to utilize the self-guided portion of the course on Compassion U for participants to complete individually before sessions. When considering how to schedule CBCT for Mental Health, the committee members will need to work with designated leadership team members to ensure client and staffing needs are balanced to provide a safe and therapeutic structure for the sessions.

Training Compassion for Mental Health

Want to Bring CBCT to Your Organization?

Visit *compassionu. app/ for-organizations*

Training Compassion for Mental Health is the full CBCT for Mental Health course. This course involves moving through a sequence of eight modules. Each module strengthens a particular skill or insight, and the modules build on each other to foster greater resilience and compassion.

Training Compassion for Mental Health should begin with a session focused on an introduction to CBCT for Mental Health, which allows teachers to cultivate buy-in and motivation for participants while clarifying

Training Compassion for Mental Health (16–24 hours)

Brief Description: A deep dive into the eight CBCT modules, tailored for those with mental health symptoms and/or diagnoses. Each module introduces new content, reflective exercises, and practices designed to strengthen inner skills and insights and support their application into everyday life.

The Training Compassion for Mental Health course is offered through Compassion U, a user-friendly app that delivers CBCT course content and provides access to instructional videos, activities, practices, and a compassion community, among other resources.

Courses include live sessions with other participants, facilitated by certified CBCT teachers and licensed mental health professionals. These live sessions are typically one hour each and occur weekly over nine weeks. Prior to each live session, participants engage in the self-guided content, activities, and practices on Compassion U. The self-guided portion of CBCT for Mental Health is the consistent component, conducted virtually for all participants. The live sessions may be offered virtually or in person and are recommended to last one hour each. As organizations envision how they can bring CBCT for Mental Health to clients, they will have to examine how in-person sessions versus virtual sessions may benefit clients.

Format:

▶ Self-guided on digital e-learning platform, Compassion U (8–16 hours, typically 1.5 hours per week)

▶ Live sessions in person or via videoconference, facilitated by a certified CBCT teacher and licensed mental health practitioner (9 hours of live sessions, typically 1 hour per week)

processes and expectations. By helping clients explore how CBCT for Mental Health can benefit them as individuals within the introduction session, teachers can aid participants in establishing personalized goals while building collaborative connections between participants. An additional consideration is for teachers to offer supplementary live sessions to give participants additional time discussing and exploring content to comprehend and internalize the concepts more fully. Some participants may need additional time to process concepts, address mental health stressors that arise when exploring these concepts, and apply the material in a more personalized manner. A sense of flexibility and curiosity is recommended for CBCT for Mental Health committee members and organizational leaders as they determine what format of CBCT for Mental Health is most efficient and effective for their programming.

Creating CBCT for Mental Health Group Rituals

CBCT for Mental Health is a practice that is done independently with reflection for self-growth, while also allowing for interpersonal connection via Compassion U and classroom sessions. While participating in Compassion U, participants may desire to create their own rituals and routines for beginning their practice, so they have established intentions and routines for participating in CBCT for Mental Health. The entire cohort may decide to create a ritual that everyone participates in before beginning any CBCT work to create a more cohesive, connected, and aligned community. Rituals to start each class might include offering tea, engaging in a settling practice, stretching, or holding space for informal connections.

Support Staff and Manage Implementation Needs

Organizing a recurring class within mental health programming takes a good amount of flexibility, patience, and consideration for all individuals involved. Supporting this work is critical for success.

Clinicians may struggle to manage the myriad mental health and/or behavioral health needs that arise while teaching CBCT for Mental Health. A CBCT for Mental Health teacher may need support or consultation with other CBCT for Mental Health teachers or clinical supervisors to have space to reflect and determine the best path for responding to a participant's needs in the group and potentially for follow-up care.

Considerable mental health needs that may arise in a CBCT for Mental Health class could look like:

- Trauma flashbacks or dissociation
- Ruminating thought patterns
- Increased feelings of distress or anxiety
- Irritability or short temper
- Feeling overwhelmed or unable to cope

Individual clinicians and organizations should be aware of the ways in which participants who have a moderate to significant trauma or mental health history may be impacted by sitting with and examining ruminating or distressing thought patterns, or the process in which a participant will have to work toward showing themselves compassion and empathy and accepting their imperfection. This can be a challenging process for individuals with mental health needs, and teachers should be prepared to offer additional care within a class or as a follow-up to a participant after the class has concluded. As organizations implement CBCT for Mental Health, they must analyze how teachers can support participants, and how teachers can be supported and given resources to succeed in the process.

"II was heading up the implementation of [CBCT] across our site, and after running two pilot groups, I went to a weekly staff meeting to talk about what they felt had gone well and what they felt and inefficient. Everyone was able to come to an agreement that the staff really did have too much on their plates and lessening the rigidity of what needed to be done and when would help everyone feel more compassionate in their roles—and allow clients more time to participate in the CBCT programming."

—CBCT FOR MENTAL HEALTH CERTIFIED TEACHER AND
   PROGRAM DEVELOPER

CBCT for Mental Health Across Multiple Programs or Sites

The approach taken to successfully implement CBCT for Mental Health in one program may not be the same for implementing at another, even within the same organization. Staff training, group formatting, and implementing CBCT for Mental Health may need to change from department to department, based on the scheduling, staff availability, and programmatic needs.

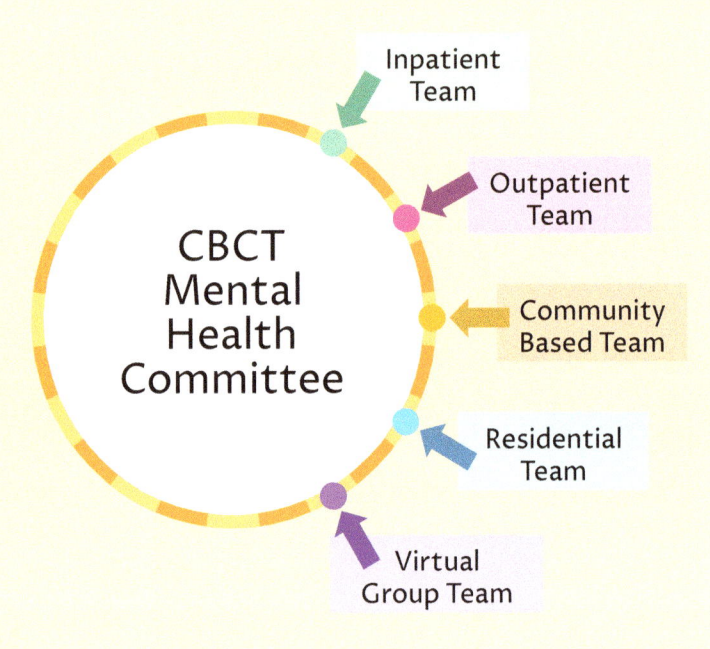

If you are scaling CBCT across multiple programs, the recommendation is to work through the process with each program specifically. Determining readiness factors is a good place to start when developing the process and approach to CBCT implementation. Recognizing strengths and barriers will support organizations in utilizing current systems, structures, and personnel most effectively.

When implementing CBCT for Mental Health across multiple sites, it is ideal to have a central CBCT committee with representation from each program- or department-based CBCT committee. This way, each program will have the capacity to share implementation techniques that have been effective or challenges they have faced in order to receive feedback and support from colleagues with mutual goals. The team can also align methods (data measurement tools, measuring outcomes, communication and messaging plans, community events, etc.) to support consistency.

This graphic illustrates a central teaming model. The CBCT for Mental Health committee includes representation from each component of programming involved in implementing CBCT for Mental Health within an organization. Having a central committee allows for adequate representation and communication of needs for all aspects of programming.

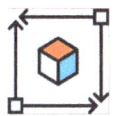 ## Plan the Physical Space

When exploring CBCT for Mental Health for your programming, planning for a space where clients will be able to examine their inner thoughts peacefully and from a non-judgmental lens without interruption is critical. Mental health clinicians cultivate their spaces, no matter how small, to represent the work that will be conducted, and to represent the peace and structure that a client can expect. Examining what spaces are available within your organization to create or develop into a CBCT for Mental Health class room or meditative space will allow clients and colleagues to move into CBCT sessions with intentions and expectations. Maintaining a thoughtfully designed space will allow clients to feel more open to engaging in reflection, delving deeper into thoughts and feelings, and participating in the therapeutic process without distraction.

 ## Document and Assess

Many mental health–serving organizations collect data on client functioning to assess the effectiveness of treatment and ensure clients receive the care they need. By tracking assessment tools that explore feelings around compassion, mental health symptoms, and overall functioning, organizations can evaluate how clients are responding to engaging in CBCT for Mental Health. This data allows teams to make informed decisions, adjust program design, and consider options for offering Mental Health for CBCT. Furthermore, understanding a client's functioning helps mental health professionals identify areas of improvement, address emerging concerns, and ensure that the treatment is aligned with the client's goals. Ongoing assessment ensures that clients are on the path to wellbeing and improves the quality of compassionate care they receive.

For mental health–serving organizations, collecting data is crucial for measuring the impact and success of interventions, specifically how CBCT for Mental Health improves client functioning and reduces negative symptomatology. Programs can determine what mental health outcomes they hope to impact by implementing CBCT for Mental Health, including but not limited to:

- Reduced anxiety
- Reduced depression
- Increased impulse control

- Decreased ruminating thought patterns
- Decreased emotional distress
- Increased self-compassion and compassion for others

Assessment Tools

There are many assessment tools that an organization can consider to meet their research and outcomes goals for client wellbeing and efficacy for CBCT for Mental Health. Here are a few assessment tools for consideration:

- CAMM – Child and Adolescent Mindfulness Measure
- CS – Compassion Scale
- SCS-SF – Self-Compassion Scale – Short Form
- DERS-16 – Difficulty in Emotion Regulation Scale (16-question variant)
- DTS – Distress Tolerance Scale
- PSE – Psychiatric Stress Experiences Scale
- ARI – Affective Reactivity Index
- MAP – Meaning and Purpose Scale
- LPI – Life Problems Inventory]

By gathering information on how CBCT for Mental Health affects client outcomes, organizations can evaluate the effectiveness of programming, identify patterns and trends, and make evidence-based decisions on how best to improve services. Data collection can also help organizations align with licensing requirements and secure funding, as many funding resources and accrediting bodies require evidence of program efficiency. Additionally, analyzing client data enables organizations to anticipate future programmatic needs, maximize resources, and explore new ways CBCT for Mental Health may be implemented across the organization. In this way, effective and meaningful data collection not only helps individual clients but also strengthens how CBCT for Mental Health serves your program.

Component 4
Support Ongoing Integration

 **Support Ongoing Integration**

Sustain, develop, and continuously integrate CBCT for Mental Health.

 **Integrating into System Structures**

 **Working through Barriers**

 **Monitoring and Adapting**

 **Hiring, Onboarding, and Providing Feedback to Staff**

 **Supporting Further Practice**

 Integrating into System Structures

Implementing CBCT for Mental Health into an organizational culture goes beyond personal and group practice. It also involves integrating the practices and principles into the community's systems, routines, and structures. As implementation continues, staff investment in CBCT for Mental Health is critical to its ongoing success and engagement.

Identify optimal times to integrate key practices and principles of CBCT into routines and structures.

Determining Where to House CBCT

Determining in what department or programmatic division CBCT for Mental Health programming should be housed.

- Determining if staff duties should be reassigned to include CBCT for Mental Health responsibilities.

- Do new positions need to be developed or filled, or is restructuring of current employee job descriptions sufficient for adequate staffing?

- Does CBCT for Mental Health need to be housed within clinical programming, or would another department, like development or recreational therapies, be more appropriate?

Incorporating CBCT into Meetings

Incorporating CBCT practices into the start of staff meetings, professional development meetings, donor engagement activities, new client orientation sessions, or conflict mediation meetings, including:

- Leading a grounding practice or engaging in a short CBCT insight activity and reflection.

- Providing time to share celebrations, insights, progress, and barriers to the CBCT for Mental Health implementation work.

Offering CBCT to Other Constituencies

Offering CBCT courses to other constituencies, such as client caregivers or family members, employee family members or individuals in their support systems, partner organizations, board members or community stakeholders, and system administrators.

- For groups serving family members of those involved in treatment, CBCT is a way to help build in natural supports for individuals in treatment, as their family members would be aware of and engaged in the same material they are receiving.

Incorporating CBCT into Onboarding and the Evaluation Process

Incorporating CBCT for Mental Health into an orientation or onboarding session and informing the employee evaluation process.

- The evaluation process is often challenging for practitioners; however, with a holding of self-compassion, a shared language can be used by those involved to foster a level of reappraisal that is imbued with compassion and allows team members to explore areas of growth and personal resiliency.

Applying Compassion-Based Ethics

Applying compassion-based ethics to the institution's disciplinary policies and/or to organization management or behavior management strategies. This could include processes that maximize the possibility of:

- Assuring that individuals are respected for their fundamental desire (and right) to seek wellbeing and avoid distress.

- Staying mindful of the dignity of all individuals, even difficult people and in difficult circumstances.

- Recalling that all lives have a measure of vulnerability and fallibility, and no one person or group is free of imperfection.

- Making room for dialogue, mutual understanding, and genuine human connection between all parties.

- When needed, enforcing punitive consequences without shutting off the possibility of genuine remorse, reconciliation, or forgiveness.

 # Working through Barriers

As most of us who have had the opportunity to lead the implementation of new programs know, barriers and challenges are inevitable. Identifying and addressing these barriers is key to continuing and sustaining meaningful work over time. Collaboration between colleagues, the ability to explore options for implementation, and the continued engagement and training of staff are critical to shift the organizational culture.

Time

- ▶ There is limited time in most mental health–serving systems. Barriers in terms of allocated professional development are persistent across programs. Prioritization, visible senior support, and long-term planning are key to finding the time for CBCT training. Another successful way to address the issue of time is to deliver the training in bite-sized periods of time; facilitating a 10-minute presentation can lead to interest in a 1-hour session, which may then lead to a half day workshop.

Funding

- ▶ Compensation for people's time matters and plays a key role in supporting engagement and buy-in. Staff will need continued monetary support to attend training, provide additional support outside of group time, and provide additional resources.

- ▶ To support long-term and sustainable implementation of CBCT for Mental Health, the organization may choose to build internal capacity by certifying staff as CBCT teachers. The certification process serves to deepen the practice of the participant and increases the organization's capacity to offer and embed CBCT into its culture.

Inconsistent communication

- ▶ Mental health–serving organizations often fail to provide consistent and ongoing communication about a prioritized initiative. Over time, communication may vary in terms of frequency or significance, but leadership and the CBCT committee must continue to engage the wider organizational community with CBCT expectations and updates. Through multiple forms and iterations of communication, organizational leaders must voice and message the impact, benefits, and progression of CBCT integration and training.

Competing needs

▶ Many initiatives exist within every mental health– serving organization. Organizations are required to meet the needs of a wide array of internal and external stakeholders, meet varying funding requirements, and meet new and updated treatment standards. The ability for CBCT for Mental Health to be linked and aligned to these different initiatives is critical to the success of the overall implementation.

▶ It may be beneficial for the CBCT committee to be consulted when exploring new grant opportunities, discussing new programming, or in drafting new staff responsibilities to ensure CBCT is complemented and uplifted.

▶ Regardless of the competing priorities within the organization, it is necessary to help staff see CBCT for Mental Health as a supportive and complementary effort, as opposed to one more thing to add to an already overwhelmed and depleted system.

Leadership and staff transitions

▶ Leadership and staff transitions are inevitable. Establishing a culture and climate characterized by resilience, awareness, and compassion will ensure that the transition of key staff does not undermine efforts to further CBCT for Mental Health programming, training, and integration. As an organization begins the process of implementing CBCT, leadership should be exploring ways to ensure that programming is secure and staff feel supported in their roles.

 **Monitoring and Adapting**

Compassion training requires regular and consistent reflection. Similarly, the implementation and integration of CBCT for Mental Health also requires regular and consistent reflection. Feedback on how the program is being received is essential to the program's success and for maintaining the sustained buy-in of faculty, staff, and clients. Maintaining a pulse on how the program is being received relies on ongoing monitoring. Feedback can come in the form of written feedback, formal and informal conversations, data collection, and observations. Each of these forms provides a unique and important basis of feedback that allows the programmatic and organizational leadership to gain insight into the impact that CBCT for Mental Health programming is having on the staff and clients. One important pathway for feedback can and should occur through the CBCT for Mental Health committee. As a representative committee, this group can engage staff and clients to gain meaningful insights about the experience of CBCT for Mental Health within the treatment setting.

Organizational leadership or the CBCT committee can develop recommendations to adapt and improve implementation based on the insights gained from staff and clients. They can then coordinate and provide additional training, enhance external communication, ensure representation from all departments within the committee itself, or even develop new integration strategies for CBCT practices and related activities.

 ## Hiring, Onboarding, and Providing Feedback to Staff

Integrating CBCT for Mental Health into an organization's culture depends on the members who make up the community and the support and resources provided by leadership. A key pathway for CBCT for Mental Health integration can occur through the hiring and onboarding of new staff. When hiring new staff, consider seeking out candidates who have knowledge and/or experience that correlates with a CBCT approach, including trauma-informed care, restorative practices and pedagogy, social–emotional learning, or a compassion-based lens. Look for evidence of knowledge in the applicant's letter of interest, the professional accomplishments listed on their resume, and their responses during the formal interview process. The selection of applicants who practice resilience and compassion goes a long way in sustaining an organizational culture that demonstrates a commitment to compassion.

When onboarding new staff, CBCT for Mental Health can be introduced in a variety of ways to engage employees at all levels in compassion-based care:

- **Interview:** Initiating discussion around CBCT for Mental Health and trauma-informed mental health care as a mission and value of the organization allows prospective employees to begin exploring what it would mean to work as a part of an organization that values compassion for all.

- **Orientation:** The orientation is another great opportunity to highlight or introduce the initiative and begin engagement in the practices. By providing a more in-depth introduction to CBCT for

Mental Health during all employees' orientation, the organization prioritizes and highlights the culture of compassion they are working to cultivate.

↪ **Mentorship:** Choosing skilled mentors with a high level of CBCT knowledge helps new staff understand and benefit from the culture of compassion and feel motivated to engage in the initiative or learn more.

 ## Supporting Further Practice

Once groups in the community have completed the CBCT for Mental Health training, it is important to have structures in place for them to continue engaging in and deepening their practice, individually and in community.

Encouraging Individual Practice

While often done in community, the CBCT for Mental Health practices are personal practices aimed at strengthening inner skills and capacities. This inner work is not complete in one, five, or even one hundred courses, but rather is understood as a lifelong practice—something we all continue to engage in, train, and apply throughout our lives. Finding the time and space to engage in the practices and incorporate them into busy schedules can be challenging, so encouraging and enabling practice among your provider community can make them feel supported, nourished, and motivated.

✓ Provide subscriptions to Compassion U for interested staff

✓ Create a space for relaxation and contemplative practice

✓ Integrate CBCT practice or Compassion U within the existing health and wellness programming

✓ Establish a community of practice for interested members of the community

✓ Embed services provided by Compassion U into an existing or emerging staff mentoring program

"Becoming a CBCT instructor has impacted me personally, socially, and professionally. In the last two years, my mindset has shifted from anxiousness, doubtfulness of my abilities to accomplish personal goals to a peaceful, well-balanced mindset … The time I spent reflecting on the CBCT practices added solace to my day, insights into problem solving with compassion, and, most importantly, self-care."

— Certified CBCT instructor

49

Encouraging Group Practice

Communities of practice

The CBCT committee and leadership team should provide options for staff to participate in a community of practice once they have completed the training. Individual groups may also choose to form their own communities of practice. Each community of practice may focus on different elements of the practice. Some options include meeting regularly to:

▶ **Debrief modules in sequence:** Going through the modules together, taking time on their own to engage in the formal and informal practices, and then debriefing together in the group.

▶ **Engage in insight activities:** Revisiting CBCT insight activities, engaging in them as a group, and then debriefing.

▶ **Engage in formal practices:** Engaging in the formal practices as a group.

▶ **Share and apply:** Engaging in informal sharing about which CBCT skills and insights have been most meaningful or most challenging or them in their work recently.

Mentoring and accountability groups

Through working together in pairs or small groups to ensure accountability and provide mentoring, staff can commit to practices and check in with each other around progress and challenges. They can ask and answer questions that may arise within this work. These groups would meet at regularly scheduled intervals to review the informal practice section of a chosen module and select one or more practices to bring the skills to life. Participants will then share what they are working on with their accountability partner(s) and check in periodically.

Conclusion

Mental health needs, symptoms, and diagnoses are varied and can manifest in myriad ways, while the resources for support and services have always been limited. Mental health providers are continuously working to ensure their treatment methods are aligned in meeting the overall treatment needs of their clients. CBCT for Mental Health offers organizations and providers the opportunity to engage in compassion-promoting practices designed to contribute to the flourishing of both clients and providers.

This guide presented a step-by-step process for integrating CBCT for Mental Health into an organization's current treatment regimen and options for programming considerations. The process outlined here draws from the experiences of other mental health–serving programs and incorporates best practices, allowing for flexibility and adaptation to meet each organization's specific needs. As organizations expand and grow over time, continual assessment and tailoring to foster engagement, commitment, and sustained growth are necessary for maintaining CBCT for Mental Health programming and contributing to a culture of compassion.

For those who embark on this meaningful journey, know that the Emory Compassion Center will be there to support you as much as possible, and that there is a growing network of mental health providers across the world—therapists, counselors, psychologists, coaches, doctors, direct-care staff, administrators, researchers, and others—who are pioneers in the field of compassion and care. As the network grows, the potential of each individual organization to make a difference will also grow, and each individual voice will become amplified. With sustained effort and mutual support, and with humility and self-compassion, this community will contribute to a more compassionate and ethical world for all.

Keep In Touch

Visit:
compassionu. app/ for-organizations

Email:
partnerships. cbct@emory.edu

Appendix A

Implementing CBCT for Mental Health: Sample Three-Year Path

Implementing CBCT for Mental Health requires intentional planning, authentic leadership, and a commitment to cultural transformation. By following this four-component framework—Establish Leadership and Vision, Cultivate Collaborative Engagement, Implement the Training, and Support Ongoing Integration—organizations can embed compassion-based practices into their practices and procedures, creating lasting benefits for staff, clients, and the broader community.

This appendix outlines a feasible three-year implementation timeline for CBCT for Mental Health, mapped to four key components of organizational integration. Each phase builds upon the last, ensuring strong leadership, staff engagement, effective training delivery, and sustainable program integration.

Sample Timeline Summary

Timeline	Component	Key Milestones
Months 0–6	Establish Leadership and Vision	Explore CBCT for Mental Health; Build Initial Support; Engage Leadership; Form the CBCT for Mental Health Committee
Months 6–18	Cultivate Collaborative Engagement	Deliver Initial Training and Gather Feedback; Select Teacher Certification Cohort; Expand Engagement Beyond Staff
Month 18–Year 2	Implement the Training	Pilot CBCT for Mental Health Groups; Expand Data Collection and Assessment; Sustain and Grow Resources
Years 2–3+	Support Ongoing Integration	Expand CBCT Organization-Wide; Embed CBCT in Organizational Systems; Secure Long-Term Funding; Plan for Expansion

Establish Leadership and Vision

Months 0–6

Key Steps and Milestones

Explore CBCT for Mental Health

- Medical director (Adam) researches compassion-based approaches online and discovers CBCT for Mental Health via Emory University's Center for Contemplative Science and Compassion-Based Ethics.
- Adam subscribes to Compassion U, completes CBCT for Mental Health himself, and experiences firsthand the program's value.

Build Initial Support

- Adam meets with his CEO to propose exploring CBCT as a program development project.
- Financial administrator is consulted to identify initial funding opportunities (e.g., professional development funds, anticipated grants).
- Adam gives a 10-minute presentation on CBCT to leadership, using template slides from Emory.

Engage Leadership

- Leadership team decides CBCT aligns with their mission and agrees to move forward with early training for leadership and supervisory staff.
- Leadership team plans and schedules an eight-week CBCT for Mental Health course for upper/middle management and clinicians.

Form the CBCT for Mental Health Committee

- Adam and clinical program director (Amy) are asked to co-chair the committee.
- Committee members are selected, including leadership, clinicians, and key stakeholders.

Cultivate Collaborative Engagement

Months 6–18

Key Steps and Milestones

Deliver Initial Training and Gather Feedback

- The eight-week leadership and staff course concludes with highly positive feedback from participants.
- Concerns are noted from direct-care staff about scheduling adjustments, and from administrators regarding long-term funding.

Select Teacher Certification Cohort

- With grant funding secured, six staff (five therapists plus Adam) enroll in CBCT-certified teacher training.
- Leadership adjusts schedules to provide six hours per week for certification homework during work hours.
- Certification training is completed over the summer and fall.

Expand Engagement Beyond Staff

- Development team discusses long-term funding strategies with Amy and Adam.
- Community engagement director and grants writer begin seeking additional funding and adding CBCT for Mental Health to donor campaigns.
- CBCT items are added to the organization's online wish list.

Implement the Training

Months 18–Year 2

Key Steps and Milestones

Pilot CBCT for Mental Health Groups

- CBCT committee meets biweekly to plan pilot implementation.
- Two pilot groups are selected. Staff and clients receive presentations explaining the new schedules, daily meditations, and wellbeing surveys.
- Direct-care staff feedback is incorporated into updated scheduling and technology plans (e.g., new iPads purchased).

Expand Data Collection and Assessment

- Adam and Amy collaborate with performance quality improvement and data analysts to integrate compassion measures into client intake and discharge surveys.
- Ongoing evaluation begins, with early data showing client improvements in emotion regulation and non-reactivity.

Sustain and Grow Resources

- Development team applies for and secures two out of three grants, funding CBCT for two years.
- Leadership agrees to fund Compassion U subscriptions for clients as part of programming expenses.

Support Ongoing Integration — Years 2–3 and beyond

Key Steps and Milestones

Expand CBCT Organization-Wide

- After six months of piloting, Adam and Amy present outcome data and a budget plan to leadership.
- Leadership approves organization-wide implementation.
- CBCT committee presents at an all-staff meeting and conducts focus groups to gather staff input.

Embed CBCT in Organizational Systems

- CBCT for Mental Health is added to new hire orientation with a partial-day training session.
- Compassion practices are integrated into disciplinary procedures, client assessments, and employee evaluations.

Secure Long-Term Sustainability

- Development team expands grant searches and secures five-year funding for CBCT for Mental Health through a mix of grants, capital campaigns, and donor bequests.
- Leadership feels confident in ongoing program viability and views CBCT as a cornerstone of organizational culture.

Plan for Expansion

- In Year 3, the CBCT committee begins exploring opportunities to offer CBCT to clients' family members.

Appendix B

CBCT for Mental Health Committee Toolkit

The CBCT for Mental Health Committee plays a vital role in guiding the implementation process, ensuring organizational alignment, and supporting sustainability. This toolkit provides templates, guiding questions, and practical resources to assist organizations in forming, managing, and empowering their committee throughout the four components of implementation.

This toolkit includes:

- Sample Committee Charter
- Sample Meeting Agenda Templates
- Initial Planning Meeting Agenda
- Ongoing Implementation Check-In Agenda
- Sustainability and Evaluation Agenda
- Key Questions for the Committee to Consider
- Sample Stakeholder Engagement Plan
- Best Practices for Committee Success

Sample Committee Charter

CBCT Committee Charter (Sample)

Purpose

The CBCT for Mental Health Committee will oversee the strategic planning, implementation, and evaluation of CBCT for Mental Health within the organization. The committee ensures alignment with organizational values, explores potential resources, and serves as a communication bridge between leadership, staff, and external stakeholders.

Objectives

- Develop and monitor the implementation plan.
- Identify and address logistical, cultural, and financial barriers.
- Support the engagement of staff and leadership.
- Guide program evaluation and sustainability efforts.

Meeting Frequency

- Twice a month during initial implementation.
- Monthly during organization-wide rollout.
- Quarterly or every other month for ongoing integration and sustainability.

Membership

- Co-Chairs: Typically program leaders (e.g., medical director, clinical program director, supervisorial clinical staff).
- Members:
  - Certified CBCT teachers in the organization.
  - Representatives from leadership, direct-care staff, and administrative teams.
  - Stakeholders from quality improvement, data analysis, and development teams.
  - Optional external advisors (e.g., community engagement specialists, board members).

Decision-Making Process

- Decision-Making Process
- Decisions will be made collaboratively, with an emphasis on committee member and leadership consensus, supported by data and stakeholder feedback.

Sample Meeting Agenda Templates

Initial Planning Meeting Agenda

- Welcome and introductions
- Overview of CBCT for Mental Health and organizational goals
- Review of committee purpose and goals
- Initial identification of key priorities
  - Vision alignment with organizational mission
  - Stakeholder mapping
  - Initial funding opportunities
- Next steps and assignment of action items

Ongoing Implementation Check-In Agenda

- Review progress on current phase (e.g., pilot group outcomes, staff or client engagement metrics)
- Identify and troubleshoot barriers (scheduling, staff concerns, client engagement)
- Update on funding and resource needs
- Plan upcoming trainings, focus groups, or community engagement events
- Assign responsibilities and set timeline for next actions

Sustainability and Evaluation Agenda

- Review data on client and staff outcomes
- Discuss integration of CBCT into onboarding, annual review, and policies
- Explore long-term funding sources and community partnerships (grants, donations, similar nonprofits, or community organizations with similar missions)
- Plan communication strategies to share successes organization-wide
- Establish goals for expanding CBCT to additional populations (e.g., family members, community partners)

Key Questions for the Committee to Consider

Leadership and Vision

How does CBCT align with our mission and existing treatment modalities?

What are our short- and long-term goals for CBCT implementation?

Collaborative Engagement

How can we foster buy-in across all levels of staff?

What stakeholders (internal and external) should we involve in planning and implementation?

Training Implementation

What is our capacity for sending staff through CBCT Teacher Certification?

How can we best schedule CBCT groups for staff and clients?

What technology or infrastructure adjustments are needed?

Ongoing Integration

How can CBCT be embedded into staff onboarding and professional development?

What systems will we use to evaluate success and adjust as needed?

How will we secure sustainable funding over the next 3–5 years?

Sample Stakeholder Engagement Plan

Stakeholder Group	Engagement Strategy	Timeline
Leadership Team	Present implementation plan and expected outcomes	Month 1
Direct-Care Staff	Host orientation sessions, gather feedback	Months 2–3
Clients and Families	Provide information sessions and materials	Prior to pilot rollout
Development Team	Collaborate on funding proposals and campaigns	Ongoing
External Partners	Share success stories, build support	Post-pilot, Year 2

Best Practices for Committee Success

✓ *Ensure diverse representation from across the organization.*

✓ *Set clear roles and expectations for each member.*

✓ *Establish a regular meeting schedule and stick to it.*

✓ *Use data and staff/client feedback to inform decisions.*

✓ *Celebrate milestones to maintain momentum and morale.*

Notes

1   Pace, T. W. W., Negi, L. T., Adame, D. D., Cole, S. P., Sivilli, T. I., Brown, T. D., Issa, M. J., & Raison, C. L. (2009). Effect of compassion meditation on neuroendocrine, innate immune and behavioral responses to psychosocial stress. *Psychoneuroendocrinology*, 34(1), 87–98. https://doi.org/10.1016/j.psyneuen.2008.08.011; Pace, T., Negi, L., Donaldson-Lavelle, B., Ozawa-de Silva, B., Reddy, S., Cole, S., Craighead, L., & Raison, C. (2012). Cognitively-Based Compassion Training reduces peripheral inflammation in adolescents in foster care with high rates of early life adversity. *BMC Complementary and Alternative Medicine*, 12(Suppl 1), 175. https://doi.org/10.1186%2F1472-6882-12-S1-P175; Pace, T. W. W., Negi, L. T., Dodson-Lavelle, B., Ozawa-de Silva, B., Reddy, S. D., Cole, S. P., Danese, A., Craighead, L. W., & Raison, C. L. (2013). Engagement with Cognitively-Based Compassion Training is associated with reduced salivary C-reactive protein from before to after training in foster care program adolescents. *Psychoneuroendocrinology*, 38(2), 294–299. https://doi.org/10.1016/j.psyneuen.2012.05.019; Reddy, S., Negi, L., Dodson-Lavelle, B., Ozawa-de Silva, B., Pace, T., Cole, S., Raison, C., & Craighead, L. (2013). Cognitive-based compassion training: A promising prevention strategy for at-risk adolescents. *Journal of Child and Family Studies*, 22(2), 219–230. http://dx.doi.org/10.1007/s10826-012-9571-7; Titanji, B. K., Tejani, M., Farber, E. W., Mehta, C. C., Pace, T. W., Meagley, K., Gavegnano, C., Harrison, T., Kokubun, C. W., Negi, S. D., Schinazi, R. F., & Marconi, V. C. (2022). Cognitively Based Compassion Training for HIV immune nonresponders—An attention-placebo randomized controlled trial. *Journal of Acquired Immune Deficiency Syndromes*, 89(3), 340–348. https://doi.org/10.1097/QAI.0000000000002874.

2   Lang, A. J., Casmar, P., Hurst, S., Harrison, T., Golshan, S., Good, R., Essex, M., & Negi, L. (2017). Compassion meditation for veterans with posttraumatic stress disorder (PTSD): A nonrandomized study. *Mindfulness*, 11(1), 63–74. https://doi.org/10.1007/s12671-017-0866-z; Mascaro, J. S., Kelley, S., Darcher, A., Negi, L. T., Worthman, C., Miller, A., & Raison, C. (2016). Meditation buffers medical student compassion from the deleterious effects of depression. *Journal of Positive Psychology*, 13(2), 133–142. https://doi.org/10.1080/17439760.2016.1233348.

3   Mascaro, J. S. et al. (2016).

4   Lang, A. J. et al. (2017).

5   Reddy, S. et al. (2013).

6   Desbordes, G., Negi, L. T., Pace, T. W., Wallace, B. A., Raison, C. L., & Schwartz. E. L. (2012). Effects of mindful-attention and compassion meditation training on amygdala response to emotional stimuli in an ordinary, non-meditative state. *Frontiers in Human Neuroscience*, 6, 292. https://doi.org/10.3389/fnhum.2012.00292; Mascaro, J. S. et al. (2016).

7   Mascaro, J., Rilling, J., Negi, L. T., & Raison, C. (2012). Compassion meditation enhances empathic accuracy and related neural activity. *Social Cognitive and Affective Neuroscience*, 8(1), 48–55. https://doi.org/10.1093/scan/nss095

8   Gonzalez-Hernandez, E., Romero, R., Campos, D., Burychka, D., Diego-Pedro, R., Baños, R., Negi, L., & Cebolla, A. (2018). Cognitively-Based Compassion Training (CBCT) in breast cancer survivors: A randomized clinical trial study. *Integrative Cancer Therapies*, 17(3), 684–696. https://doi.org/10.1177/1534735418772095; Sun, S., Pickover, A. M., Goldberg, S. B., Bhimji, J., Nguyen, J. K., Evans, A. E., Patterson, B., & Kaslow, N. J. (2019). For whom does Cognitively Based Compassion Training (CBCT) work? An analysis of predictors and moderators among African American suicide attempters. *Mindfulness*, 10(11), 2327–2340. https:// doi.org/10.1007/s12671-019-01207-6; Titanji, B. K. et al., (2022).

9   Nakao, M., Shirotsuki, K., & Sugaya, N. (2021). Cognitive-behavioral therapy for management of mental health and stress-related disorders: Recent advances in techniques and technologies. *BioPsychoSocial Medicine*, 15(1), 16. https://doi.org/10.1186/s13030-021-00219-w

10 Beck, J. S., & Fleming, S. (2021). A brief history of Aaron T. Beck, MD, and cognitive behavior therapy. *Clinical Psychology in Europe*, 3(2), 1–7. https://doi.org/10.32872/cpe.6701

11 Robins, C. J., & Chapman, A. L. (2004). Dialectical behavior therapy: current status, recent developments, and future directions. *Journal of Personality Disorders*, 18(1), 73–89. https://doi.org/10.1521/pedi.18.1.73.32771

12 Dimeff, L., & Linehan, M. M. (2001). Dialectical behavior therapy in a nutshell. *The California Psychologist*, 34(3), 10–13.

13 Substance Abuse and Mental Health Services Administration (SAMHSA). (2014). *SAMHSA's Concept of Trauma and Guidance for a Trauma-Informed Approach.* https://library.samhsa.gov/sites/default/files/sma14-4884.pdf

14 Van der Kolk, B. A. (2014). *The Body Keeps the Score: Brain, Mind, and Body in the Healing of Trauma.* New York: Viking.

15 Gilbert, P. (2014). The origins and nature of compassion focused therapy. British Journal of Clinical Psychology, 53(1), 6–41. https://doi.org/10.1111/bjc.12043

16 Millard, L. A., Wan, M. W., Smith, D. M., & Wittkowski, A. (2023). The effectiveness of compassion focused therapy with clinical populations: A systematic review and meta-analysis. *Journal of Affective Disorders*, 326, 168–192. https://doi.org/10.1016/j.jad.2023.01.010

17 National Alliance on Mental Illness (NAMI). (2023). Mental health by the numbers. https://www.nami.org/about-mental-illness/mental-health-by-the-numbers/

18 NAMI. (2023).

19 McGrath, J. J., Al-Hamzawi, A., Alonso, J. et al. (2023). Age of onset and cumulative risk of mental disorders: a cross-national analysis of population surveys from 29 countries. *The Lancet Psychiatry*, 10(9), 668–681. https://doi.org/10.1016/S2215-0366(23)00193-1

20 McGrath, J. J. et al. (2023).

21 Thiagarajan, T., & Newson, J. (2022). *The Mental State of the World in 2022.* The Mental Health Million Project. https://mentalstateoftheworld.report/wp-content/uploads/2023/02/Mental-State-of-the-World-2022.pdf

22 Nigam, J. A., Barker, R. M., Cunningham, T. R., Swanson, N. G., & Chosewood, L. C. (2023). Vital signs: Health worker-perceived working conditions and symptoms of poor mental health – quality of worklife survey, United States, 2018– 2022. *Morbidity

and Mortality Weekly Report, 72(44), 1197–1205. https://doi.org/10.15585/mmwr.mm7244e1

23 Nigam, J. A. et al. (2023).

24 SAMHSA. (2022). *Addressing Burnout in the Behavioral Health Workforce through Organizational Strategies*. https://library.samhsa.gov/sites/default/files/pep22-06-02-005.pdf

25 Dowling, T. (2018). Compassion does not fatigue! *The Canadian Veterinary Journal = La revue veterinaire canadienne*, 59(7), 749–750.

26 Maguen, S., & Norman, S. (2022). Moral injury. National Center for PTSD: *PTSD Research Quarterly*, 33(1). https://www.ptsd.va.gov/publications/rq_docs/V33N1.pdf

27 The National Child Traumatic Stress Network (NCTSN). (2025). Secondary traumatic stress. https://www.nctsn.org/trauma-informed-care/secondary-traumatic-stress

28 Aguilar-Raab, C., Winter, F., Warth, M., Stoffel, M., Moessner, M., Hernández, C., Pace, T. W. W., Harrison, T., Negi, L. T., Jarczok, M. N., & Ditzen, B. (2023). A compassion-based treatment for couples with the female partner suffering from current depressive disorder: A randomized-controlled trial. *Journal of Affective Disorders*, 342, 127–138. https://doi.org/10.1016/j.jad.2023.08.136

29 Lang, A. J. et al. (2017).

30   Herbert, M. S., Liu, L., Malaktaris, A., Kamura, K., Casmar, P., & Lang, A. J. (2022). Compassion meditation for veterans with PTSD: home practice matters. *Mindfulness*, 13, 2315–2323. https://doi.org/10.1007/s12671-022-01959-8

31 Reddy, S. et al. (2013).

32 Dodds, S. E., Pace, T. W. W., Bell, M. L., Fiero, M., Negi, L. T., Raison, C. L., & Weihs, K. L. (2015). Feasibility of Cognitively-Based Compassion Training (CBCT) for breast cancer survivors: a randomized, wait list controlled pilot study. *Support Care Cancer*, 23(12):, 3599–3608. https://doi.org/10.1007/s00520-015-2888-1

33 Pace, T. W. W. et al. (2009); Reddy, S. et al. (2013).

34 LoParo, D., Mack, S. A., Patterson, B., Negi, L. T., & Kaslow, N. J. (2018). The efficacy of Cognitively-Based Compassion Training for African American suicide attempters. *Mindfulness*, 9(6), 1941–1954. https://doi.org/10.1007/s12671-018-0940-1

35 Lang, A. J. et al. (2017).

36 Titanji, B. K., Tejani, M., Farber, E. W., Mehta, C. C., Pace, T. W., Meagley, K., Gavegnano, C., Harrison, T., Kokubun, C. W., Negi, S. D., Schinazi, R. F., & Marconi, V. C. (2022). Cognitively Based Compassion Training for HIV immune nonresponders—An attention-placebo randomized controlled trial. *Journal of Acquired Immune Deficiency Syndromes*, 89(3), 340–348. https://doi.org/10.1097/QAI.0000000000002874.

37 Aguilar-Raab, C. et al. (2023).

38 Flückiger, C., Del Re, A. C., Wampold, B. E., & Horvath, A. O. (2018). The alliance in adult psychotherapy: A meta-analytic synthesis. Psychotherapy, 55(4), 316–340. https://doi.org/10.1037/pst0000172